PHOTOSYNTHESIS

By Harriet Brundle

BookLife
PUBLISHING

©2019
BookLife Publishing
King's Lynn
Norfolk PE30 4LS

All rights reserved.
Printed in Malaysia.

A catalogue record for this
book is available from the
British Library.

ISBN: 978-1-78637-467-7

Written by:
Harriet Brundle

Edited by:
Holly Duhig

Designed by:
Jasmine Pointer

Photocredits:

Images are courtesy of Shutterstock.com. With thanks to Getty Images, Thinkstock Photo and iStockphoto.
Front cover - Aphelleon, Tim UR, Madlen, Ian 2010, Robyn Mackenzie, ILYA AKINSHIN, Nella, Kriengsuk Prasroetsung. 2- HanZign. 3 – Nella.
4 – Singkham. 5 - Joe Belanger. 6 – showcake. 7 - Irina Markova. 8 - ulrich22. 9 - idiz. 10 - Lubomir Chudoba. 11 - Bachkova Natalia. 12 – LouieLea.
13 - Bobkeenan Photography. 14 – SergeyIT. 15 – OMMB. 16 – DaCek. 17 - PISUTON'c, tanaphongpict, Serjio74, Rich Carey, NuntekulPhotography,
JIANG HONGYAN, Valentina Razumova, givaga, Eric Isselee, Ekaterina V. Borisova, Anan, Kaewkhammu, Maks Narodenko. Tim UR, Jim Cumming.
18 - Yuliya Evstratenko. 19 - Marten_House. 20 - Juli_17. 21 - Volodymyr Burdiak. 22 - Bucha Natallia, gnohz. 23 - all_about_people, EsHanPhot.

Items should be returned on or before the date shown below. Items not already requested by other borrowers may be renewed in person, in writing or by telephone. To renew, please quote the number on the barcode label. To renew online a PIN is required. This can be requested at your local library.
Renew online @ **www.dublincitypubliclibraries.ie**
Fines charged for overdue items will include postage incurred in recovery.
Damage to or loss of items will be charged to the borrower.

Leabharlanna Poiblí Chathair Bhaile Átha Cliath
Dublin City Public Libraries

Comhairle Cathrach
Bhaile Átha Cliath
Dublin City Council

Due Date	Due Date	Due Date

CONTENTS

Words that look like <u>this</u> can be found in the glossary on page 24.

ALL ABOUT FOOD

Plants need water, air, sunlight, warmth and <u>nutrients</u> in order to grow and stay alive. All plants need these things and without any one of them, they may not be able to survive.

Healthy plants usually have leaves of some kind.

All plants need water. Some plants need more than others. A cactus, for example, can survive with a small amount of water.

You are a living thing and you need food to give you energy so you can move and grow. Plants are able to make their own food, so they don't need to eat dinner like you or me!

PLANTS

Plants come in lots of different shapes and sizes. Some plants grow on land while others grow in water. Once they begin to grow from a seed, lots of plants have roots which keep them in one place.

Roots are like straws which take water and nutrients from the soil.

Roots

Plants grow in the sea, rivers, lakes and lots of other places too!

Different plants live in a range of different <u>habitats</u>. Some plants live in extremely hot and dry places while others prefer wet and cold surroundings. A plant will usually grow well if it has the right <u>conditions</u>.

WHAT IS PHOTOSYNTHESIS?

Photosynthesis (say: fo-toe-sinth-eh-sis) is the process of a plant making its own energy. Plants need three important things in order to photosynthesise: light from the Sun's rays, <u>carbon dioxide</u> and water.

Photosynthesis happens in the leaves of plants.

Some plants cannot photosynthesise if the weather gets too hot.

Plants take in the carbon dioxide they need through their leaves and the water through their roots. When the Sun shines on a plant's leaves, photosynthesis will happen.

HERBIVORES AND OMNIVORES

Herbivores are animals that only eat plant matter. Herbivores enjoy eating a range of different plants including grass, leaves and seeds. Antelope, sheep and giraffes are all herbivores.

For herbivores to survive, there must be plenty of plant matter for them to eat.

Some birds eat both berries and worms.

Omnivores are animals who have a diet of both plant matter and meat. Omnivores often have more of a varied diet than other animals because there are lots of different foods they can eat.

PLANT PROTECTION

With hungry herbivores and omnivores on the lookout for delicious plant matter to eat, lots of plants have had to develop different <u>features</u> which help them avoid being eaten.

This koala is feasting on a plant.

Holly leaves are sharp, which can put animals off eating them.

Some plants have spiky parts which dig into an animal if they get too close while others can cause a sting if you touch them. Some berries and other plants are <u>poisonous</u> if they are eaten.

THE FOOD CHAIN

A food chain is a series of plants and animals which all need each other to survive. At the start of every food chain is a plant, which is also known as a producer.

Animals that eat plants or other animals are called consumers.

Cows are consumers.

If a plant were to die,
a whole food chain
might be affected.

Plants are called producers because they make their own food and this is why they start off the food chain. All the animals further up the food chain need the producer in order to survive.

Lots of food chains that link together are known as a food web.

After producers come herbivores and omnivores, which are animals that eat plants. The last step in the food chain is always an omnivore or carnivore. Carnivores are animals that only eat meat.

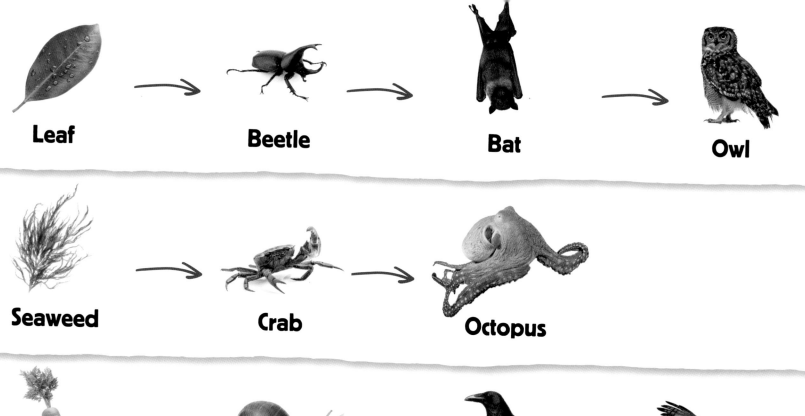

Leaf → **Beetle** → **Bat** → **Owl**

Seaweed → **Crab** → **Octopus**

Carrot → **Snail** → **Crow** → **Hawk**

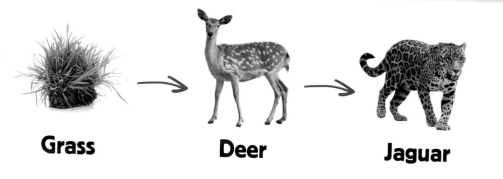

Grass → **Deer** → **Jaguar**

The arrows in a food chain show the direction the energy is moving. Every chain starts with a plant!

Fruit → **Raccoon** → **Coyote**

PRECIOUS PLANTS

One of the reasons plants are very important is because, when they photosynthesise, they release oxygen. Oxygen is a <u>gas</u> that humans and animals need to breathe to survive.

Plants take in carbon dioxide, which is a gas that can be harmful to our planet.

When lots of trees are cut down, it is called deforestation.

Lots of plants and trees are being cut down every day to make space for new homes and farmland, and so that the wood can be sold. This is bad for our planet.

Plants are also important because they are home to lots of different animals. One tree could be home to insects, birds and animals such as squirrels and bats.

In some countries, you might see a monkey in a tree.

If one animal dies, it can affect the whole food chain.

When plant matter is cut down, some animals could lose their habitat or lose their source of food in that area. This can cause animals to die or have to move to a new area where they wouldn't normally live.

POWERFUL PLANTS

Did you know that different types of plants are used for <u>medicine</u>? Other plants, such as lavender, can be used to help people relax.

Lavender

Coast Redwood

One of the world's tallest trees is a coast redwood, which measures over 115 metres high!

Lots of people suffer with hay fever, which is caused by the <u>pollen</u> from plants. Hay fever can make your nose run and your eyes feel itchy.

Venus Fly Trap

There are some carnivorous plants that eat animals such as flies to top up on energy!

GLOSSARY

carbon dioxide	a gas found in the air
conditions	the different things needed for plants to grow, such as light
features	important or interesting parts of something
gas	air-like
habitats	homes of plants or animals
medicine	used to treat and stop illness
nutrients	needed for life and growth
poisonous	something which can cause death or illness
pollen	a powder made by plants

INDEX